To

From

D0590472

Other books in this series:
HAPPY ANNIVERSARY
To a very special BROTHER
To a very special DAD
To a very special DAUGHTER
To a very special FRIEND
To a very special GRANDDAUGHTER
To a very special GRANDMA
To a very special GRANDPA
To a very special GRANDSON

Wishing you HAPPINESS
To my very special HUSBAND
Someone very special…
    TO THE ONE I LOVE
To a very special MOTHER
To a very special SISTER
To a very special SON
Wishing you happiness
    FOR YOUR WEDDING

Published in 1993 by Helen Exley Giftbooks in Great Britain.
This edition published in 2008

12 11 10 9 8 7 6 5 4 3 2 1

ISBN 13: 978-1-84634-299-8

Illustrations and design © Helen Exley 1993, 2008
The moral right of the author has been asserted.
A copy of the CIP data is available from the British Library on request.

Acknowledgements: The publishers are grateful for permission to reproduce
copyright material. While every effort has been made to trace copyright holders,
Exley Publications would be pleased to hear from any not here acknowledged:
Roger McGough, "Happiness", copyright 1973 by the author, from Gig, published
by Cape 1973. Reprinted by permission of the author and publishers; Edwin Muir,
"The Confirmation", from Collected Poems, Faber and Faber Ltd. Reprinted by
permission of the publishers. John Steinbeck: "7/12/43 letter to Gwyndolyn
Steinbeck" by John Steinbeck, from STEINBECK: A LIFE IN LETTERS by Elaine A.
Steinbeck and Robert Wallsten, editors, copyright 1952 by John Steinbeck, © 1969
by The Estate of John Steinbeck, © 1975 by Elaine A. Steinbeck and Robert Wallsten
Used by permission of Viking Penguin, a division of Penguin Group (USA) Inc.
Printed in China.
'TO A VERY SPECIAL'® IS A REGISTERED TRADE MARK OF HELEN EXLEY GIFTBOOKS

Helen Exley Giftbooks, 16 Chalk Hill, Watford, Herts WD19 4BG, UK
www.helenexleygiftbooks.com

To my very special
WIFE

EDITED BY HELEN EXLEY
ILLUSTRATIONS BY JULIETTE CLARKE

No cord or cable can draw so forcibly,

or bind so fast,

as love can do with a single thread.

ROBERT BURTON (1577-1640)

HELEN EXLEY®

SHE

She gave me eyes, she gave me ears, and
humble cares, and delicate fears, a heart, the fountain
of sweet tears. And love, and thought. And joy.
WILLIAM WORDSWORTH (1770-1850)

I love her from the hairs on her head to the soles
of her feet, and that includes all the funny,
beautiful, strange and intriguing bits in between.
RICHARD ALAN

The greatest and richest good.
My own life to live in. This she has given me.
ARCHIBALD MACLEISH (1892-1982)

Above all she has given me herself to live for!

Her arms are able to hold me up against the world:

her eyes are able to charm away every care;

her words are my solace and inspiration....

THOMAS WOODROW WILSON (1856 - 1924)
TO HIS WIFE ELLEN

...he without her is but

half himself. She is his absent hands, eyes, ears

and mouth; his present and absent all...

a husband without her is a misery

to man's apparel....

SIR THOMAS OVERBURY (1581-1613)

My golden child, my pearl, my precious stone,

my crown, my queen. You dear darling of my heart,

my highest and most precious, my all and

everything, my wife, the baptism of my

children, my tragic play, my posthumous reputation.

Ach! You are my second better self....

HEINRICH VON KLEIST (1777-1811)
TO ADOLFINE HENRIETTE VOGEL

REAL LOVE

I learned the real meaning of love.
Love is absolute loyalty.
People fade, looks fade, but loyalty never fades.
You can depend so much on certain people,
you can set your watch by them.
And that's love, even if it doesn't seem
very exciting.
SYLVESTER STALLONE

The supreme happiness of life
is the conviction of being loved
for yourself, or, more correctly, being loved
in spite of yourself.
VICTOR HUGO (1802-1885)

Familiar acts are beautiful
through love.
PERCY BYSSHE SHELLEY (1792-1822)

Left alone, Levin asked himself
again if he really felt any regret
for the freedom his friends had been
talking about. The idea made
him smile. "Freedom?
What do I need freedom for?
Happiness for me consists
in loving, in thinking
Kitty's thoughts and wishing
her wishes,
without any freedom."

LEO TOLSTOY
FROM "ANNA KARENINA"

A GOOD MARRIAGE

The married state, with... the affection suitable
to it, is the completest image of heaven
and hell we are capable of receiving in this life.
RICHARD STEEL (1672-1729)

What is there in the vale of life
Half so delightful as a wife,
When friendship, love, and peace combine
To stamp the marriage bond divine?
WILLIAM COWPER

A marriage makes of two fractional lives a whole;
it gives to two purposeless lives a work,
and doubles the strength of each to perform it.
MARK TWAIN (1835-1910)

I think a man and a woman should choose
each other for life, for the simple reason
that a long life with all its accidents is barely
enough for a man and a woman to understand
each other; and in this case to understand
is to love.
JOHN BUTLER YEATS

A good marriage is that in which each appoints
the other guardian of his solitude.
RAINER MARIA RILKE (1875-1926) FROM "LETTERS"

hen one has once fully entered the realm of love,
the world – no matter how imperfect
– becomes rich and beautiful,
for it consists solely of opportunities for love.
SOREN KIERKEGAARD (1813-1855)

MY HEART'S FRIEND

Fair is the white star of twilight,

And the sky cleaner at the day's end;

But she is fairer, and she is dearer,

She, my heart's friend!

Fair is the white star of twilight,

And the moon roving to the sky's end;

But she is fairer, better worth loving,

She, my heart's friend.

SHOSHONE LOVE SONG

HAPPINESS

Lying in bed of a weekday morning

Autumn

and the trees

none the worse for it.

You've just got up

to make tea toast and a bottle

leaving pastures warm

for me to stretch into

in his cot

the littlefella

outsings the birds

Plenty of honey in the cupboard.

Nice.

ROGER McGOUGH

COME LIVE WITH ME

Come live with me, and be my love,

And we will some new pleasures prove

Of golden sands, and crystal brooks,

With silken lines, and silver hooks.

JOHN DONNE (1573-1631)

As you are woman, so be lovely,
As you are lovely, so be various,
Merciful as constant, constant as various,
So be mine, as I yours for ever.
ROBERT GRAVES (1895-1985)

I will give my love an apple without e'er a core,
I will give my love a house without e'er a door,
I will give my love a palace wherein she may be,
And she may unlock it without any key.

My head is the apple without e'er a core,
My mind is the house without e'er a door,
My heart is the palace wherein she may be,
And she may unlock it without any key.
FOLK SONG

We rest so calmly; we lie so warmly;

Hand within hand, as children after play....

JOHN LEICESTER WARREN, LORD DE TABLEY (1835-18⁹
FROM "SIGH, HEART, BREAK NOT"

Happiness is being snug abed with the person
you love – and the rain lashing
the window and drumming on the roof. Safe.
PETER GRAY, b. 1928

What in the world is better than to wake up early
and find the room aglow with first light...
and to turn to one another under the blankets,
knowing it is Sunday Morning.
BRIAN E. WILLIAMS, b. 1961

Although I conquer all the earth,
yet for me there is only one city.
In that city there is for me only one house;
And in that house, one room only;
And in that room; a bed.
And one woman sleeps there,
The shining joy and jewel of all my kingdom.
FROM THE SANSKRIT

ALL FOR YOU

She is mine to have and to hold!
She has chosen between love and gold
All the joys life can give
Shall be hers, while I live,
For she's mine to have and to hold.

WILL A. HEELAN

To believe in a woman,
to make her your
religion, the fount of life,
the secret luminary
of all your least thoughts –
is this not second birth?

HONORÉ DE BALZAC

...As for me, to love you alone,
to make you happy, to do nothing
which would contradict your wishes,
this is my destiny
and the aim of my life.
Be happy, do not concern yourself
about me; do not interest yourself
in the happiness of a man
who lives only in your life,
who enjoys only your
pleasures, your happiness.
When I require from you love such as mine,
I do wrong... When I sacrifice to you
all my desires, all my thoughts,
all the moments of my life, I
yield to the ascendancy which your charms,
your character, your whole being has gained
over my wretched heart.

NAPOLEON BONAPARTE
FROM A LETTER TO JOSEPHINE

A PEACE, A CALM

There is no happy life

But in a wife;

The comforts are so sweet

When they do meet:

'Tis plenty, peace, a calm

Like dropping balm....

WILLIAM CAVENDISH (1592-1676)

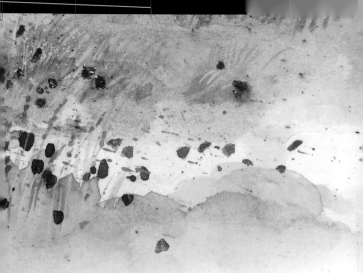

When a man of thirty-five is happily,
blissfully married, the scope of his reflections
is necessarily limited... He is no longer haunted
by the face of every pretty girl he meets,
for he has already met the woman most fitted
in the wide world to make him happy...
He is no longer prone to dreams
about the object of his affections,
for he has her perpetually beside him.

ROBERT GRANT
FROM "REFLECTIONS OF A MARRIED MAN", 1892

UNCHANGING LOVE

If twenty years were to be erased and I were
to be presented with the same choice again
under the same circumstances I would act
precisely as I did then...

Perhaps I needed her even more in those
searing lonely moments when I – I alone
knew in my heart what my decision must be.

I have needed her all these twenty years.

I love her and need her now.

I always will.

DUKE OF WINDSOR
ABOUT HIS WIFE

I'll love you dear, I'll love you
Till China and Africa meet,
And the river jumps over the mountain
And the salmon sing in the street.

I'll love you till the ocean
Is folded and hung up to dry
And the seven stars go squawking
Like geese about the sky.

W. H. AUDEN

You ought to trust me for I do not love and will
never love any woman in the world but you,
and my chief desire is to link myself to you
week by week by bonds which shall ever become
more intimate and profound.
Beloved I kiss your memory – your sweetness
and beauty have cast a glory upon my life.

SIR WINSTON CHURCHILL (1874-1965)
FROM A LETTER TO HIS WIFE, CLEMENTINE

WITHOUT HER

Without her laughter a room full
of babbling people feels cold and empty.

N. NAIDOO

They all think I'm tough, successful,
even macho. Only she knows. I'm weak,
I'm like a lost puppy without her.

HUGH COTTRELL

I can pack just as well as she can.
But she doesn't forget my tooth-brush.

PETER SIMONS

Without Judy
I'd suddenly feel forty-one years,
two months and eleven days old,
after all.

ROBERT NORTH

BEING WITH YOU

Being with you is like walking
on a very clear morning –
definitely the sensation of belonging the
E.B. WHITE (1899-1985)

True Love is but a humble, low-born thir
And hath its food served up in earthen wa
It is a thing to walk with, hand in hand
Through the everydayness
of this workday world.
JAMES RUSSELL LOWELL (1819-1891)

Love from one being to another
can only be that two solitudes come nea
recognize and protect and comfort each o
HAN SUYIN, B.1917

How very good it is to have shared
life with you, to have weathered
storms together. To have shared quiet
times and laughter.
PETER GRAY, B. 1928

Darling, you want to know what I want
of you. Many things of course
but chiefly these.
I want you to keep this thing we have
inviolate and waiting
– the person who is neither I nor you
but us.
JOHN STEINBECK (1902-1968)
TO HIS WIFE GWENDOLYN

TOGETHER ALWAYS

When she consented to dance,

the first time I met her, I held her hand.

In cinemas, on country walks, I held her hand.

When promising to love and cherish,

I held her hand.

When each child was born,

I held her hand.

Such small hands! Golden hands!

Amazingly creative – to economize.

Hard worked and roughened they may have been

but only smoothness was sensed in her caressing

Now the hands are blue-veined, drawn

white but still active. Cool on my fevered

head, warm and comforting when

I am down. And if we go to the church or

shop, in fact anywhere I always hold that

precious hand.

GEORGE SOMERVILLE

I'd choose her again anytime, anywhere. Put her in a crowd of beautiful, intelligent girls and I'd choose her. That's because she's good for me and ·r tum doesn't put my middle-age spread to shame.

DAVE MASON

She runs her fingers through my hair
like she did when we were courting even though
I've only three left.

A. BOURNE

Grow old along with me! The best is yet to be,
The last of life, for which the first was made.

ROBERT BROWNING (1812-1889)